How to Do Nothing with Nobody All Alone by Yourself

How to Do Nothing with Nobody All Alone by Yourself

by Robert Paul Smith

Illustrations by Elinor Goulding Smith

Tin House Books

First published by W. W. Norton and Company 1958
Published by Tin House Books 2010

Parental Advisory: This book describes activities that may be dangerous if not done exactly as directed or that may be inappropriate for young children. All of these activities should be carried out under adult supervision only. The author's estate and the publisher expressly disclaim all liability for any injury or damages that may result from engaging in the activities contained in this book.

Published by Tin House Books, Portland, Oregon, and New York, New York
Distributed to the trade by Publishers Group West, 1700 Fourth St., Berkeley, CA 94710, www.pgw.com

Library of Congress Cataloging-in-Publication Data

Smith, Robert Paul.
  How to do nothing with nobody all alone by yourself / by Robert Paul Smith. — Tin House Books ed.
    p. cm.
  Originally published: New York : Norton, 1958.
  ISBN 978-0-9820539-5-9
  1. Amusements. I. Title.

GV1203.S63 2010
793—dc22

                    2009037103

Printed in the USA
Interior design by Janet Parker and Justin Lucero

www.tinhouse.com

For Nathalie,
who ate my spinach

Nothing Doing

I don't know about you, but I wasted all but about fifteen minutes of my childhood. Those fifteen minutes were spent on a beach in Cornwall busting a nodule of quartz out of a fist-sized chunk of flint; thirty years later, I still have it somewhere in my office, in an old coffee can. Everything else I made during those years—the swords nailed together from pickets, the forest forts that defended nothing from nobody, the poorly assembled Revell model cars with Testors paint smeared lazily on them, the Sherman tanks drawn in near-medieval 2-D perspective—they're all gone now.

Come to think of it, I haven't used the piece of quartz for much either.

But if I want reminding of where the rest of that time went, I have this book. A step-by-step guide to grinding oyster shells against the front stoop for no reason, to turning buttons and string into buzz saws that won't cut anything, and to making paper boomerangs that don't come back, *How to Do Nothing with Nobody All Alone by Yourself* is about what you do when you're a kid and have neither money nor anyone paying much attention to you, and where your one guiding principle is that you avoid grown-ups and don't ask for help.

"Objects made of wood by children," Smith once estimated, ". . . will assay ten percent wood, ninety percent nails." And if his book's title also works on the same principle of youthful overengineering, it's because a belief in *efficiency* and *quality construction* is anathema to childhood. Waste rules—and what Smith knows is that if youth is wasted on the young, it's because an adult would not waste it, and in so doing make it *not* youth.

"These days," he writes, "you see a kid lying on his back and looking blank and you begin to wonder what's wrong with him. There's nothing wrong with him, except he's thinking . . . He is trying to arrive at some conclusion about his thumb."

So why not carve monkeys out of peach pits? Why not build a tank out of spools and rubber bands, or a paddleboat out of cigar boxes? Why not make pussy-willow cats up on the fence?

"If things were as they should be, another kid would be telling you how to do this," Smith admits. But Smith was just about the best guide America had to precious arcana like making a game of "killers" out of the horse chestnuts in your backyard. If Jean Shepherd had written *The Dangerous Book for Boys* instead of *A Christmas Story*, this book would be it. And like Shepherd, Smith had a history in broadcasting, one that began in Manhattan in the late 1930s as a radio writer at CBS. "This paid the rent," he recalled, "while I wrote four novels which did not." After penning bohemian novels about Greenwich Village, and cowriting a play that improbably went on to star Frank Sinatra in the movie version, it was marriage and fatherhood that inspired Smith's meditation upon the lore of his childhood. The illustrations by his wife, Elinor—an accomplished author herself—makes for a book truly created by the Smith household. It seems fitting that he later wrote a book about "household possessions they don't make anymore"—old cast-offs like carpet beaters, wooden iceboxes, and hat stands. After all, every kid also wonders about the junk in the attic, and Smith always remembered what it was like to be a kid.

That's why *How to Do Nothing with Nobody All Alone by Yourself* remains timeless. Toys are louder and brighter now—and a good deal safer than Smith's old games of mumbly-peg—but kids still do nothing the same way. They pick up the random and discarded object of adult life, or the natural debris that no one with a job or a schedule or *things to do* even notices anyway. Kids will find this stuff, examine it, flip it upside down, throw it, break it, and simply stare at it. Kids will do nothing with nobody all alone by themselves. And you get a sense, after Smith's magisterial symposium on making helicopters out of rubber bands and chicken bones, that there is something more at stake in all this.

"I understand some people get worried about kids who spend a lot of time alone," Smith muses in his closing lines, "... but I worry about something else even more; about kids who don't know how to spend any time all alone, by themselves." Doing nothing with nobody, and doing it well, is a talent at living.

—*Paul Collins*

If things were as they should be, another kid would be telling you how to do these things, or you'd be telling another kid. But since I'm the only kid left around who knows how to do these things—I'm forty-two years old, but about these things I'm still a kid—I guess it's up to me.

These are things you can do by yourself. There are no kits to build these things. There are no classes to learn these things, no teachers to teach them, you don't need any help from your mother or your father or anybody. The rule about this book is there's no hollering for help. If you follow the instructions, these things will work, if you don't, they won't. Once you have built them my way, you may find a better way to build them, but first time, do them the way it says.

First thing is a spool tank. For this you need an empty spool. Here's one place your mother can be ootzed into the deal. You can ask her for a spool. If she hasn't got an empty one, you'll have to wait until she does. In the meantime, build something else.

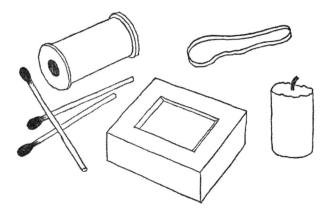

Okay, now you've got the spool. You will also need a candle or a piece of hard soap, a rubber band, and three or four large wooden kitchen matches. If you want to be real fancy and you've got a thumbtack, that's okay, but you don't really need it, and it's really not the right way to build a spool tank. The first thing to do is make the washer. Take a kitchen knife or your jackknife. We used, sometimes, to hold the blade under the hot water until it got fairly warm, thinking it would make it easier to slice the candle, but I've just tried it, and I honestly don't think it makes any difference. You can try it both ways and see. Either way, what you do is cut a slice of candle, from the bottom of the candle. Cut it fairly thick, at least a quarter of an inch. The finished washer doesn't have to be that thick, but it's easier to cut a thick slice of the candle than a thin slice without its breaking. If the candle, when you cut it, looks as if it's made in thin layers, like an onion, forget it. You'll never get a decent washer out of it. Either find the kind of candle that's made solid, or use soap. If you find the right kind of candle, keep cutting slices until you get a good solid one. You may find it easier to pull the slice off the candle without cutting through the wick, leaving a hole. If you cut right through the wick, with one of your matches push out the little piece of wick in the center if it's still there. Now go outside and find a very smooth stone, like a sidewalk, and rub, gently, until the washer is nice and flat on both sides. You don't really need a stone, you can do it on a wooden floor, if your mother is somewhere else.*

* The other night a friend of mine, who lived only six blocks away when we were kids, told me that he used to make the washers out of the paraffin that used to be on the top of jars of homemade jam. *Now* he tells me!

If you use soap, cut a slice with your knife—you don't have to heat the blade for soap—and then trim it round, and then poke a hole in the center, with the punch on your knife, or you can even do this with the matchstick too. With the matchstick, rub a little groove in the washer, or cut the groove carefully with your knife.

Then thread a rubber band through the hole, and put the matchstick through the loop it makes. Now work the rubber band through the spool. It's too short? Get a longer one. It's too long? Double it. Now break off a piece of another matchstick and put it through the rubber-band loop at the other end of the spool.

Wind it up, and then put it down. It will run across the floor, it will climb a considerable slope, and if it runs ahead of itself so the stick is in front instead of in back, just wait. The stick will come slowly up and over and when it touches the ground, you're in business again.

If you've wound it and it doesn't go because the washer won't turn, without taking the tank apart rub the washer against the spool just where it is. If the little matchstick at the other end skitters around, jam pieces of matchstick in the hole like this or use a thumbtack.

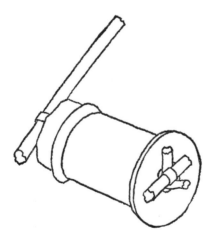

If you're interested in making a real climber out of it, cut little notches all the way around the rims of the spool and that will give it a good grip.

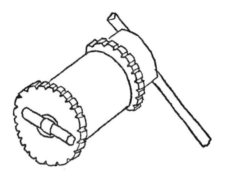

Of course, once you know how to do it, now that I've told you, you can teach another kid, and then you can have races or hill-climbing contests, or just plain fights between your tank and his.

Another thing we used to do was make what we called a button buzz saw. This is something you can make in about five minutes any time you've got nothing special to do. First you have to find a button, the bigger the better. It's got to be the kind that doesn't have a shank, but two or four holes like this.

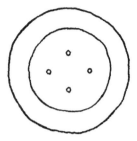

Get some dental floss or fishline or any kind of thin strong string, and put a loop through like this.

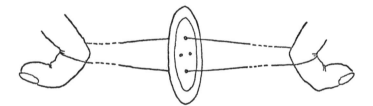

The dotted lines are because there isn't room on the page, but the loop should be about a foot long.

Now put your two index fingers—those are the ones you use for pointing—through the loop like in the picture and twirl the button until you've got the string twisted on both sides of the button. Then pull. The string will unwind and seem to get longer. Just before there's no more slack in the string, loosen it by bringing your hands together. The button will wind up the other way, and you just keep on doing this. It will feel as if the string is a rubber band. This is because it's twisting and getting shorter, untwisting and getting longer, and of course when it twists one way the button goes around in one direction, and when it twists the other way, the button reverses. If you hold the button, while it's going around, up against a piece of stiff paper, say the cover of a magazine that's sticking out over the end of a table, it'll make a kind of siren noise. I can't tell you exactly how to do this, it's kind of a matter of feel, but after a while you'll find you can make the button not only go around, but it will travel, while going around, first towards one hand and then the other. You probably know how to use a yo-yo, and this is the same general idea, but we didn't know about yo-yos, because there weren't any yo-yos to know about then.

By the way, as long as we're talking about spools and buttons: it's entirely possible that you won't find either a spool or a button of the right size around your house; when I was a kid, all mothers sewed and eventually there was an empty spool, and when clothes wore out, mothers used to cut the buttons off before they threw the clothes away, and save them in a big box. But as I say, that doesn't always happen any more, and if you can't find a button or a spool at home, take a walk and go to the tailor shop, or cleaning store, or whatever they call it in your town or neighborhood. As I said this book is things you do yourself; so don't ask your mother to do this. That's against the rules. Go yourself and ask the man in the store. And if you're really lucky—I never was—there's a kind of spool that's used on great big factory sewing machines, about the size of a can of peaches. If you get one of these, get a really big rubber band (you'll probably have to buy it—when we were kids and wanted big rubber bands, we used to cut them out of an old automobile tire inner tube, but lots of tires don't have tubes any more). Instead of matchsticks, use pencils, and if your mother makes jelly herself, you know about the big disk of wax that's on top. If she doesn't make jelly, and if she makes jelly and doesn't use wax, cut a great big washer out of soap.

Now I'll tell you how to make a handkerchief parachute. For this you'll need an old handkerchief—it's got to be an old one, that you or your father don't use any more—some string, and a stone, or some washers. Lay the handkerchief out flat.

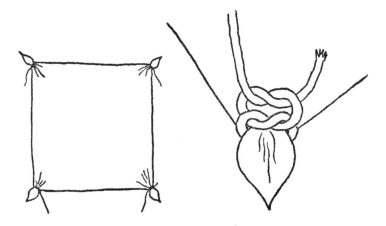

Now take a piece of string, cut it into four pieces, each about a foot long, and tie one piece around each corner. Twist up the corner and tie a square knot. That's right over left, left over right.

Pull the strings out straight so the corners of the handkerchief are all together. Now take all four strings and tie a knot about three or four inches up from the bottom. We used to hunt around and find a stone with a kind of dent in the middle, so you could tie the string around tight. But we rarely found a good stone, and it almost always comes loose sooner or later, and then I found a box in the basement that had a lot of heavy washers in it. If you can find washers, it's better. You put the string through the holes

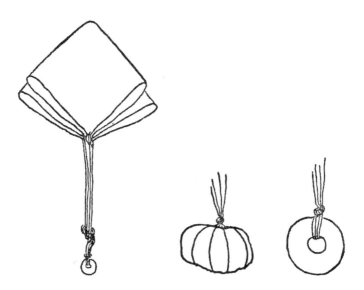

and tie it up tight. If all you've got is a stone, tie it the best you can, in all directions.

Now take the center of the handkerchief between your thumb and index finger and whirl it around and around, until it's going good. You can tell it's going really good when you hear it make a kind of whistling noise. Let go of it when the stone is coming up. The stone will carry it up in the air, then it will start to fall, stone first, the handkerchief will open out like a parachute, and there you are. Lots of times it will get caught in a tree or on a telephone wire. What do you do then? If you can climb a tree, you climb the tree. If it's on a telephone wire, you do *not* climb the telephone pole, because maybe it's also an electric light pole, and the kind of electricity that runs in those wires is very dangerous. If you threw it in a tree that's too tall, or if it's a telephone wire, build another parachute.

While we're at handkerchiefs, we used to make blackjacks out of them. Not real blackjacks, not heavy or hard enough to injure anybody, but they were pretty good for fighting. You could catch a kid a pretty good shot with one, and he could thump you pretty good, but they didn't do any real harm. Take a handkerchief and lay it out flat. Fold it in two, and then again.

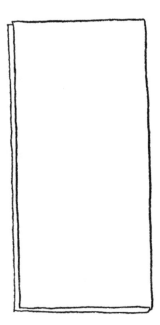

Now take the three top corners all together and roll up the handkerchief like this.

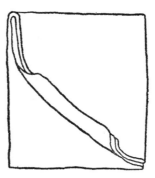

Keep rolling all the way to the top and then over, then pull at the lump until it's good and tight.

There were a couple of fairly idiotic things we used to do when we were just sitting around in the grass, which you might find fun. First, how to make a squawker out of a blade of grass. Get a good wide blade, put it between your thumbs like this,

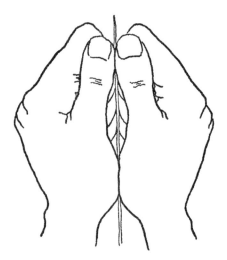

and blow. It makes a pretty loud noise, and you can make the noise higher or lower depending on the width of the blade and how tight you make it.

Also, sprawling on the grass you're sure to find dandelions. Everyone knows about blowing the white feathery things off, but one thing we used to do was to take the stem, make a slit with our thumbnail at one end, and pop it in and out of our mouths until the split pieces curled up like this.

Like I say, it's fairly idiotic, but kind of fun. And we're not through with the dandelion yet. If you pinch off one of the leaves at the stem, then push your thumbnail in it about an inch above, a little way in but not all the way through, you can pull the two sections apart leaving the little white threads in between like a little violin. The trick of course is to see how long you can get the strings without busting them, and how many of them.

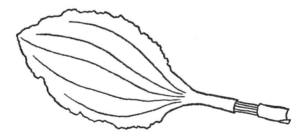

You may or may not know about burrs, and what you can do with them. I'm not going to waste a lot of time telling you how to find a burr bush. The way we found them was we'd be walking through some brush, and if you do, then burrs find you. They'd be stuck to our sweaters, our stockings, everywhere. They feel sticky to the touch, but they're not. They have dozens, maybe hundreds of little tiny hooks all over them, with very fine points, so fine they stick right into your skin without hurting you.

Burrs will stick to anything, including other burrs. You can shape them into any shape you want. We used to make baskets out of them, line them with green leaves and use them to carry berries home in.

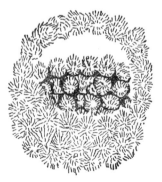

Sooner or later, however, what we did with burrs was throw them at each other. If they get into a girl's long hair, they can be a nuisance to get out, and don't ever throw a whole ball of them. They can hurt. There's another kind of burr, shaped like this:

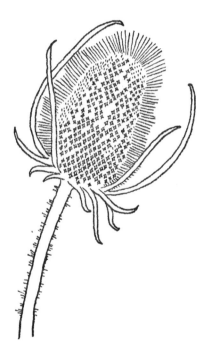

We never found a use for them, but they were kind of nice to look at. By the way, in the old days, when my grandfather was a kid, these were used for finishing off homespun woolen cloth, to bring up the nap.

You may have noticed by now that the things in this book don't come in any sort of order; that some of the things I've told you about are for indoors, some for outdoors, some for spring and some for fall and some for winter: as I told you before, you're not supposed to do all the things in this book in order: when you've got the spool, build the spool tank. When you've got the burrs, make a burr basket. I think the best way to use this book is just to read it through once, and then put it somewhere where you can find it when you want it. And then one day, when you've got nothing special to do, hunt out an old handkerchief and make the parachute. Or find a button and make the buzz saw. But read the book through once. At the back, I'll put an index so that you can find out what you want when you want it.

One thing you're sure to have any old time is a pencil; and here are two things we always did with pencils, as soon as we owned a pocketknife. Right now, before I tell you about the pencils, let's have a little straight talk about a knife. *I* don't know how old you have to be before you get a pocketknife; that's up to your father. If you ask your mother, it'll probably turn out that *she* thinks you ought to be twenty-one before you can have one. I think you'll be able

to work out something reasonable with your father. Well, let's assume you've got the knife. Now, a Boy Scout knife is swell for mumbly-peg, a game which I'll tell you about later. But for whittling, and for all sorts of *making* things, a plain old-fashioned penknife is the best. Personally, I like a small knife. You can hold it better and control it better. It's my opinion that all you need in a penknife is one, or at most, two blades. The kind I like has a horn handle, and the blades are shaped like the one on this page. This one is drawn about full size. (Of course you'll never have both blades open at once—This is just to show you the kind of knife.)

Now, here's something else that you're just going to have to argue out with your mother; I did with my mother, my kids did with their mother. A sharp knife is safer than a dull knife. A sharp knife cuts more easily, you don't have to use as much force on it, and you can control it. Nobody can do good work with a dull knife—and ask any carpenter, nobody can do safe work with any dull tool.

Now, it's got to be a good knife to be sharp. Nobody can put a good edge on a poor knife. A good one will cost more than a cheap one, but it's worth it. It'll take a good edge, it will hold it, and it will last practically

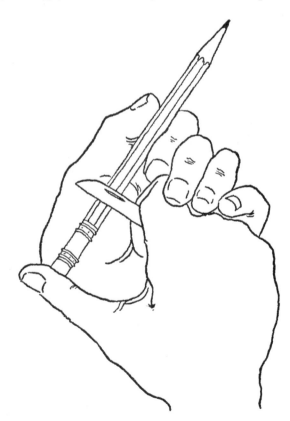

forever. When I was a kid, we all thought the only good knife was a Case knife. They still make them, they're still good knives; there are lots of other good knives, but I know about Case. You should learn how to sharpen a knife. For that you need an oilstone. We used to sharpen knives by taking a flat stone, spitting on it, and then sharpening it, but it isn't as good as an oilstone. There are lots of books that will tell you how to sharpen all kinds of tools. They'll be in your library, but the best way is to get someone who knows how to show you. In any case, the reason I mentioned the Case knife is that ever since I've known about it, the factory has guaranteed that if you will send the knife back to them at any time, they'll sharpen it and send it back to you. And they do a swell job.

Okay, that's it about knives. Now, let's say you have the knife and you know how to use it, and you have a pencil.

One of the things we did was to cut a thin strip at the top of the pencil. Then we took a pen and wrote our names or initials on it, very small, like this.

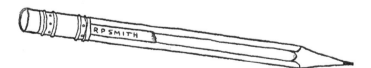

I know that you can get pencils with your names stamped on them, but we didn't have them then, and somehow it's different when you do it yourself.

Another thing we did was to decorate our pencils by cutting. Take one of the hexagonal pencils (hexagonal means six-sided, as a square is four-sided). These are usually painted yellow. Now, cut a very thin sliver, like this, so you've lifted off a little square of paint. Now on the side

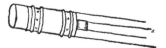

of the pencil right next to the side you've cut, cut another little square of paint that you can sliver off. Now the next

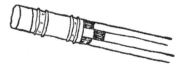

side, and so on all around the pencil, making a checkerboard effect.

Working the same way, sort of, you can make a spiral all down the pencil. Or maybe you have some ideas of your own.

By the way, in the spring and summer when you can find a green branch of some kind, you can do all these things and many more with the branch. You cut very lightly, just enough to cut through the dark bark, and when you peel that off, you see just about the whitest white you'll ever see. We used to make walking sticks out of these branches, but we never really used them for walking. It was just to make designs in the bark.

If you can find a willow tree in the spring, you can make a whistle out of a willow branch, but you'll have to get a book from the library telling you how, because I never could make one.

One of the things I found out when I was writing this book was that an artist can't draw a picture of something without seeing it. I talked my wife into doing the drawings, and I've spent about a month now in making all the things in the book so that she could draw them. Fortunately for me, I was doing this in the fall, and I could tell her that the reason I couldn't make a willow whistle was because the only time to make willow whistles was in the spring. If you want the real truth, I never even *knew* a kid who could make a willow whistle. But there were books in the library that told how to make a willow whistle, and I used to try. The only reason I'm even mentioning it is that people I've talked to claimed they knew a kid when they were kids who was able to make willow whistles. Maybe I'm just a dope about willow whistles and you'll be very good at making them. But everything else in the book I've made. I made them when I was a kid, and I made them again as a grownup, and they work. This is a guarantee.

If you don't know what a willow tree looks like, go to the public library and get out a book about trees. You'll notice that all through this book, I advise you to go to the library when you want to find out something. I think just plain going to the library and getting out a book is a swell thing to do. It's something to do, when you've got nothing to do, all by yourself. It's a thing I still do when I've got nothing special to do. I just wander around until I find a book that looks interesting; let's say, a book about ship-building, or rockets, or a story by some author I've never heard of before. Now, chances are I'll never build a ship, or ride in a rocket, and maybe I won't like the way the author I never heard of writes. But it's interesting to know how someone else builds a ship, or plans to fly in a rocket, or how the author feels about things.

Now, as long as we're talking about knives, let's talk about mumbly-peg. This is a game you can play any time of the year it's not too cold or too wet to sit on the ground— which means it's really okay for any time except when there's two feet of snow or a flood.

This is the game you play with a Boy Scout knife. There's a long thin blade in it with a ridge along one side.

The blade is called an awl, and it's made for punching holes in leather and things, but when I was a kid, that blade was a mumbly-peg blade. Your father may have called it something else—I kind of remember some kids who came from another town calling it munjigo-peg, but it's the same game. I'm sure, just the way it was called a different name in different places, it's probably played a little differently in different places—but here's the way we played.

Sit down on the ground. Open up that awl blade; hold the knife flat in your palm. The idea is to flip the knife up, so it goes and sticks in the ground.

That's the first thing in mumbly-peg. Learn to do this one first, and you'll get an idea of how the knife balances and how high to throw it, and how to get your hand and knee out of the way. It's supposed to stick in the ground, not in you. Incidentally, that's another reason for using that particular blade. You notice that the tip is rounded and it doesn't have a cutting edge on it. Also, playing mumbly-peg is not the best thing in the world for

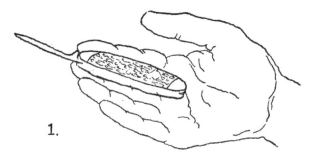

1.

a knife blade, what with hitting pebbles and dirt, and this blade is not sharp to begin with, so it can't be dulled, and that ridge along the edge strengthens it, so it won't break the way a regular knife blade might.

Now, if you're playing with another guy, you choose up to start. One of you flips the knife from the palm of the hand. If it sticks up right in the ground, that guy goes on to the second thing. If the knife doesn't stick, the other guy gets a chance to flip it from his palm. If it sticks, he goes on to the second thing. If it doesn't, it goes back to you and you try and so on. This is the way it goes on all through the game, except for one thing which I'll tell you about in a minute.

The second thing in mumbly-peg is flipping the knife, same way, only from the back of the hand, like this:

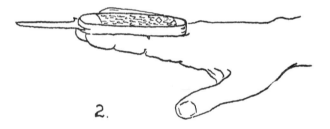

2.

Now here's the thing I said I'd tell you in a minute. Suppose you have flipped it, and it stuck, from the palm. You go on to the second thing, the back of the hand. Suppose it doesn't stick when you flip it from the back. Then you have a choice. You can take a second chance doing it from the back. If it sticks, you go on. If it doesn't, the knife goes to the other guy, *and* when it comes back to you, you have to start at the beginning. This may not seem like much of a gamble to you now, but wait until you've done ten things, and you have to make the choice between trying it again, or going all the way back ten things to the beginning.

I've been talking to people about mumbly-peg and some of them say that when they played you had to reach at least the high dive (that comes later) before you got a chance to risk—that's what we called taking a second chance, we said we'd risk. Some other people say that they couldn't risk until they got to pennies, which comes later too, and still other people can't remember. I'm one of those other people: it seems to me the people who say you can't risk until the high dive are probably right. You can make your own rules about this.

Okay; after the palm, after the back, this comes next: you make a fist, with the fingers up. You lay the knife in the groove between the tips of your fingers and the fat part of your hand. You have the blade laying over the thumb, and the idea is to bring the hand around in a circle, and stick the knife in the ground. You have to do this first with the right hand, then with the left hand. This one is hard to describe, and it sounds hard to do, but strangely enough it's one of the easiest.

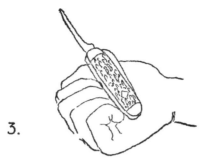

3.

Next, very much like the one above except that you bring your two middle fingers down, your two end fingers sticking out, the knife as in the drawing.

4.

This one you do right and left hand.

Now, remember, each time you get your choice of taking another shot at it if you miss, with the understanding that if you miss again, the other guy gets the knife and when you get it back from him, if and when he misses, you have to go all the way back to the beginning.

Next one is like the two before, except that you just lay the knife flat on your palm. To be sure the knife doesn't slip off, you have to bring your hand around quickly, and that's why this one comes after the two before. You'll have, by then, an idea of how to swing your hand. Incidentally: with these right- and left-hand things, they're all one. If you miss, on the left hand, next time you do it you have to do right *and* left hands.

Here's another place where the people I've been talking to don't agree. Some of them say sure, they remember this one, others say they don't. I think sometimes we did and sometimes we didn't. You see, in the days when I was a kid, you learned mumbly-peg from another kid, and the rules you learned were his rules. If he came from another part of the country, he taught you the way the kids played there: nobody, so far as I know, ever tried to write down the way to play mumbly-peg until I got stuck with the job. And believe me, the last thing in the world I want to see is an official rule book of mumbly-peg, or mumbly-peg leagues or championships. You can leave this one in, or take it out. It's your game, and you play it the way you think is right. Just be sure that when you play it with another kid, you're both playing the same game.

Now: particularly when you're doing the ones that mean you have to flip the knife over sideways, make sure the other guy is sitting across from you, not next to you, so he isn't in the way if the knife slips: and if you're the other guy, make sure you're not sitting in the way. When we were kids, we used to play it squatting, not sitting, but that's because when we were kids, if we came in with our pants dirty, we caught blue blazes. With the dungarees you kids wear, I don't know how anybody could tell if they were dirty.

The next one is pretty easy, sort of a breather after the hard ones. It's done standing up. It's called the high dive. For this, you put the point of the knife against the fat part of your hand, the little pillow of your thumb. You balance 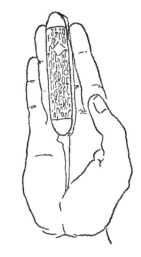 the handle back against your finger, and then tip the knife over so that it flips over and into the ground.

5.

The next one is a real cinch. I really don't know why it comes into the game this late, because you have to try pretty hard to miss this one, but this is where it comes all the same. It's called through the well. All you do is make a circle with the thumb and index finger of your left hand, and just drop the knife through.

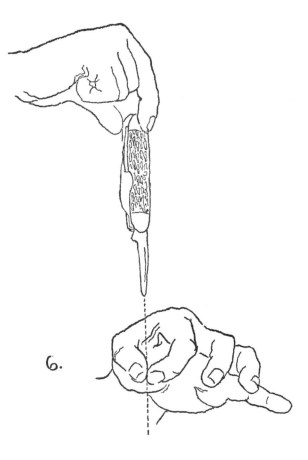

6.

Okay now, the next one is called pennies. You take the knife by the handle, rest the point of the blade on your first finger, put the first finger of the other hand on top of the knife, and flip. Same thing with point of blade on second finger, third, pinkie. Right hand first, then left hand.

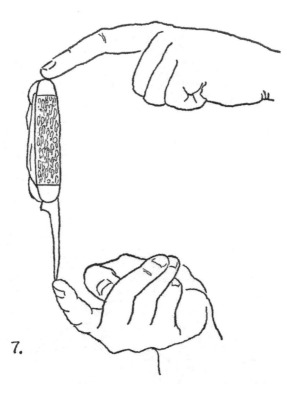

7.

The next one is called nickels. You take the knife by the blade between your thumb and first finger, and stand up. You flip it. Then between your thumb and second finger, then thumb and third finger, then thumb and pinkie. First right hand, then left hand.

Pennies and nickels are kind of tough, and very

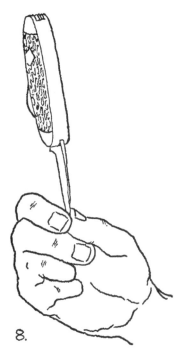

annoying, and it's here that you'll be tempted to take your second chance and miss, and find yourself all the way back at the beginning, but it's also where you'll find you do it better if you keep on going, there's a kind of rhythm to it; and it's quite a choice which to do.

All through the game, by the way, if you hit a pebble, it's a free shot,

8.

and I imagine there will be arguments about whether it hit a pebble or not. The only advice I can give you is don't holler it was a pebble if it wasn't, and if it was keep on hollering until you win. The other thing there will be arguments about is this: Sometimes the knife won't stick straight up. If it leans over, this is the rule: if you can get two fingers under it, it counts.

9.

The reason why there'll still be arguments even with the rule is that sometimes it looks as if the guy is ootzing the knife up with his two fingers. It mostly looks that way when it's the other guy, rarely when it's yourself. Anyhow, this argument, like all arguments with your equals, is something you'll learn to straighten out by yourselves.

Now that the argument about the argument is over, we go to Tony Chestnut. If you break that name into pieces, it becomes *toe, knee, chest, nut.*

Sitting down, you put your heel on the ground, the knife on your *toe*, like this.

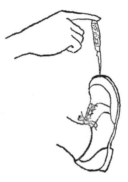

10.

Kneeling on one knee, the other like this, the knife like this, is *knee*.

11.

Chest is just the way you think.

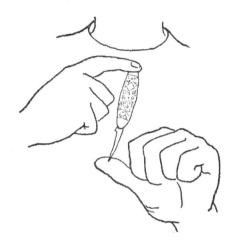

12.

Nut is just what you'd expect. Use your forehead.

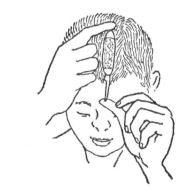

13.

And I expect that without my telling you, you have the brains to know that you have to lean over when you're doing *chest* and *nut* so that the knife sticks into the ground, not you. But since I'm not sure whether you have the brains or not, I'll tell you. Well, what do you know? I already did.

Now the next thing in mumbly-peg is Wind The Clock. You hold the tip of the blade between your thumb and index finger. With the index finger and next finger of your other hand, you hit the handle of the knife so that the knife whirls around in the air and sticks in the ground. This one is played standing up and is pretty tough to do. The reason I don't tell you how many times the knife whirls around in the air before it sticks in the ground is because I don't know. And if I did know, it would be different for me and for you and for your friend Charlie, because we're all different heights.

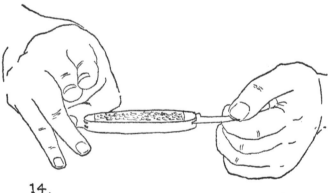

14.

Next comes Spank The Baby. This is very much like Wind The Clock, and some kids used to do one or the other, and they used to call it one or the other. We did both. What we called Spank The Baby was to put the handle of the knife in your left hand with the blade pointing toward the right hand. Hit the blade with the index finger of your right hand so it flips up and over and in.

The next one we did was called Johnny Jump the Fence. For this you stick the knife in the ground to start; that's Johnny. You put your left hand down on the ground; that's the fence. To make Johnny jump the fence you hit the

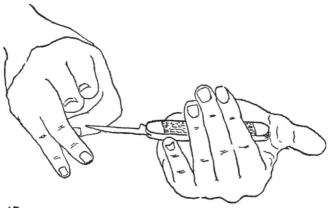

15.

knife handle with the same two fingers you used to Spank The Baby, the knife flies up in the air, over your hand and into the ground, and Johnny jumps the fence.

If you've never played mumbly-peg before, you'll think this is impossible. I'm not sure I could do it right now, because I haven't played mumbly-peg in a long time,* although there are a lot of things I do as a grownup that I'd rather play mumbly-peg than, but when I was a kid, I could do it, and so could the other kids. It's a tough one, though, maybe the toughest one in the whole game. Now here is where, after you've missed a couple of times, you'll

---

* Now I'm sure I could do it right now, because I just did. I went out in the front yard and set it up just the way the picture goes and the third time I tried, I did it. I'm still not sure I could do it right *this* minute.

want to have another try, and sometimes it's a good idea—but just remember you'll have to go all the way back to the very first thing. I used to, more often than not, take a chance on this. My friend Mitch practically never did. He grew up to be a lawyer, and I grew up to be a writer, and to this day, when I think it's time to take a chance on something, I have to go see Mitch and have him tell me whether it's a good thing to take a chance on.

The next-to-last thing in mumbly-peg is simply to flip it over your shoulder and have it stick in the ground. When I say "simply," I mean it's simple to talk about. It's hard to do.

17.

The very last thing you do in mumbly-peg is to spell O-U-T, out.

To make the "O," you make your thumb and index finger of one hand into a circle and drop the knife through. (I know this is just like "through the well," but it's an "O," too.)

To make the "U," make the same fingers into a "U" and drop it through.

To make the "T," take the knife flat on the palm of one hand with the point facing the ends of your fingers, hold out the other hand palm down, and bring the hand with the knife up and over so that the hand slaps the back of the other hand, the knife goes over and into the ground, crossing the "T." I know that sounds complicated, but look at picture 20, and if you're still not sure, get your father to show you, and if you're still not sure, try it with a pencil first until you get the idea. That might not be a bad idea to try with any of the things in mumbly-peg you're not sure of from my description.

Now, there may be one or two things I left out, but I don't think so. But if there are, stick them in the list according to how tough they are: the tougher, the further along in the list.

I said at the beginning of the book, the things in the book are things you can do all by yourself. Now mumbly-peg is a game to play with other kids. There can be two or three or four or five. More than that, it really takes too much time for the knife to go around.

But it's also a game you can play by yourself. And the rules still hold. If you miss, and take another chance

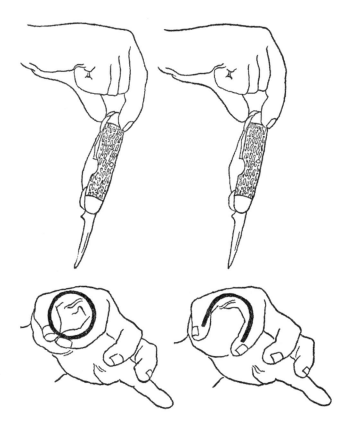

and miss again, go all the way back to the beginning. As I said, a Scout knife is good to play mumbly-peg with, but you can really play with any knife. The only thing is,

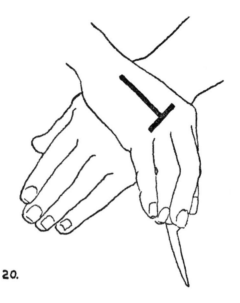

20.

if it's a knife with a sharp blade, watch what you're doing, even more carefully than with a Scout knife.

Those people are around again, telling me how *they* played mumbly-peg. Okay, they called Wind the Clock "Slice the Cheese," and I told them that on my block Slice the Cheese was something entirely different, and it had nothing to do with slicing, cheese, or mumbly-peg. I feel sure your father will show you Slice the Cheese, or maybe he calls it Slice the Ham, but I don't know how happy you'll be to learn it. And some other people tell me instead of doing O, U, T is out, the way we did it, they said O as they flipped the knife off their shoulder, U as they flipped it off the elbow, and T as they flipped it off their wrist. It seems to me some kids I knew used to do it that way, too.

Now, maybe you want to know why they call it mumbly-peg. Well, we never knew why when we were kids. It was called mumbly-peg because that was its name, like your name is Marmaduke. Much later on, I found out why. Some places, when they played, at the end of the game they cut a wooden peg the length of the winner's little finger, and sharpened it. The peg, that is, not the finger. Then each player in the game got to hit the peg with the handle of the knife, holding it by the blade, using it as a hammer. I have been told each player got to hit the peg twice, though some people tell me it was figured out in some involved way they no longer remember. In any case, you hit the peg into the ground, and the loser had to pull it out with his teeth. Of course, if you got the peg far enough into the ground, the loser had to eat a little dirt to get at the peg, and chances are when he got his mouth full of dirt, he mumbled *something*—just what, I would not care to say. So, he mumbled the peg, and the game was called mumbly-peg.

But as I say, we never did that. I'm sure we would have, if we'd known it was a way to make somebody eat some dirt. You can do that part of it or not, as you please. It all depends on how you feel about getting a mouth full of dirt.

Here's a thing we used to do in the summer, after a trip to the seashore. We always used to come back with a handful of seaweed, skate-eggs, fiddler crabs in a bucket of water, all sorts of stuff. By the way, for collecting nature stuff, there are lots of swell books, by people who know much more about it than I do. You can get them at the library, I'm sure. One in particular that I want to recommend to you is called *Handbook for the Curious,* by Paul Griswold Howes. It's put together in such a way that if you have a thing, and you don't know if it's a bug or a kind of crab or a snake or a worm—this book will tell you. There are lots of books which will tell you what kind of a bug a bug is if you know it's a bug. But this book will tell you first *if* it's a bug, and then what kind of a bug it is.

One of the things we were sure to bring home from the beach was a clamshell or two. They're nice to look at, nice to have. You can use them as little dishes, to mix paint in, make paste in,* even eat from, and if you can find a big enough one, your father will find it a handy ash tray.

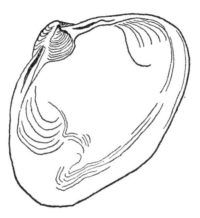

But you can make something out of it, too. If you have the kind of front stoop I used to have when I was a kid, the steps made out of concrete, that's your workbench for making clamshell bracelets. For whom? Well, for your sister, if you've got a sister, or your girl, if you've got a girl,

---

* It has been brought to my attention that some kids don't know how to make paste any more, that they think paste is only something that you can buy. With us, it was the other way around. We knew how to make it, and later on found out it was possible to buy it. Well, I'm not going to draw any pictures or give any careful instructions here. You take flour and water and mix it until it's paste, and if you have some salt you can put it in, too. I don't know if the salt does any good, but we figured we had nothing to lose. It wasn't our salt.

or if not, just for the fun of making them. You can wear them yourselves. Indians wear bracelets, why not you?

If your front steps aren't concrete, then look around. Probably the sidewalk is, or the garage floor, or a wall. It doesn't make any difference, so long as it's concrete, and the rougher the better. If you'll hold the clamshell with the rounded part down, your hand on top, and just keep rubbing, first the outside layer will wear away, and you'll see the polished shell underneath, and if you keep on rubbing, sooner or later—mostly later—you can grind a hole right through the shell. When it's big enough to get your hand in, it's a bracelet. This is something to do when you've got a lot of time on your hands.

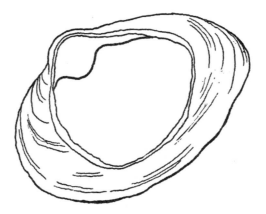

Now I'm going to tell you about another thing we made, a kind of dart, and it's my guess that when your mother or father sees it, you may catch a little hell; I don't know. I did.

So I guess right here, there better be another little speech about danger, like the one about knives. It's my belief that things themselves are not dangerous. It's the people who use them. One man driving a car is safe as houses; another is a menace to everybody on the road. I think the man who is safe is safe because he knows how to drive a car properly, and the man who is a menace is a danger because he hasn't ever really learned to drive. Sometimes the dangerous man is dangerous because he just doesn't care, which is even worse. You know kids like that, I'm sure.

But it doesn't seem to me the answer to safe driving is to do away with automobiles, nor does it seem to me any more sensible to do away with bee-bee guns because some kid you know is a dope.

I can't give you any better argument than that to use with your parents about any of the few things in this book that are dangerous; and I must say that as far as I am concerned, with my own kids, I show them how to use the dangerous things, then watch them do it themselves, and if I see they don't do it just exactly the safe way, they don't get to use the dangerous thing until they prove to me that they know how to be careful.

It's got nothing to do with age, by the way; I know kids of seven that I'd trust with a knife, and I know men of fifty that I wouldn't trust with a sharp lollipop stick.

So that's the end of the lecture, and this is how you make a needle dart. Get a thin needle from your mother. I'd suggest that you don't hook it from her sewing box, but ask her for it. Ladies are funny about needles.

Then get a burnt kitchen match. Cut or break the burned part off. Now with the thinnest blade of your knife, make a cut each way in the end of the match. It may take you a few matches before you get it done properly. Then put the needle in the center of the cross, eye-end first, and push it as far up into the match as you can. Take a little piece of thread, and wrap it around the length of the split place. The best way to do this is to smear that part of the match with glue after you've put the needle in, wrap it, and stick the ends of the thread down with glue, too. If you have airplane cement, it will dry almost as soon as you're through wrapping. Make sure the needle is as straight as you can get it.

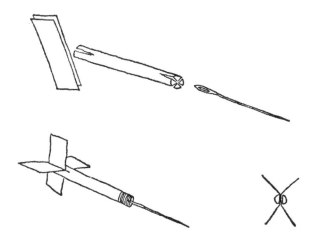

Then cut just one slit at the other end of the match, about an inch long. Cut two strips of paper, the width of the slit and twice as long. Slip them both into the match at their center point. Then bend each little piece of paper back, so that you form little wings, the way it is in the picture. I think you'll be pleased to find that this dart, used indoors, will stick to practically anything, curtains, furniture, sometimes even walls, and it does not leave a mark. I wouldn't suggest aiming it at the very best antique table in the livingroom, because even a little mark would convince your mother that the dart was dangerous.

Of course it is, and I'm here to tell you if I ever saw a kid throw one of these at another kid, there'd be a ruction in the house that wouldn't die down for a long time.

When I was a kid, there was no such thing as a suction cup—you know, the little rubber things that you have on the ends of arrows and darts, the thing that perhaps your father has to hold an extra ash tray in the car. But we did use to make something that was very much like it. We called it a leather sucker. It's a cinch to make. All you need is a piece of fairly heavy leather, but soft: not as thick as a shoe sole, not as thin as a glove. My cobbler (that's what we called shoe repairmen when I was a kid) calls it innersole leather. It's about an eighth of an inch thick, smooth on one side, rough on the other. You cut it in a circle, and the size isn't important.

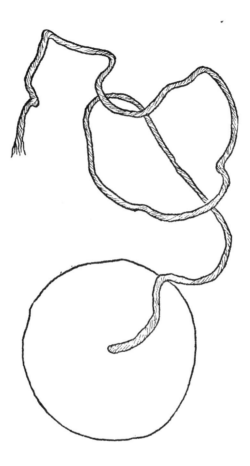

Two inches across is about as small as I ever made them and six inches is about as big. I always used them with the rough side down, but with the one I made today I found out it will work either way. It doesn't have to be a very smooth circle, either. In the center make a small

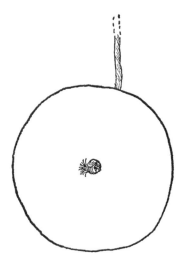

hole—the mumbly-peg blade of your knife is good for this—and put a good heavy piece of string through it and tie a good hard knot. Then put the leather to soak until it's really sopping wet and soft. Take it by the end of the string and walk around until you find a good flat stone, and drop it on the stone. Make sure the sucker is lying really flat on the stone: you may have to tap it down gently with the sole of your foot or smooth it down with your hand.

Then pull up on the string: one of three things will happen: you'll either lift the stone up, or you won't be able to pull the sucker off the stone, or you'll break the string, depending on how heavy the stone is, how strong you are, and how strong the string is. If you happen to live near a brook or stream, you'll find that's a good place to use the sucker, because there will be flat, wet stones there (it works best on stones that are at least damp), and because you'll be able to keep the sucker soaking wet there.

I built one this morning, just to be sure I remembered how they are made, and I don't live very near a stream, so I soaked mine in the kitchen sink and tried it on things in the kitchen. With a sucker two and a half inches across, I was able to lift up an iron frying pan that weighs three pounds. I managed not to drop it on my foot either. (Hope you have the same good luck.) To get the sucker off a stone or a frying pan or even the floor, don't just keep pulling up until it comes loose, because you may pull the string right through the sucker. Just lift up one edge of it and the whole thing will come loose.

What happens with the sucker is a kind of interesting thing: although you may not know it, air weighs something. It presses down on us all the time, although we don't feel it, and it presses down on everything—the ground, puppy dogs, tomatoes, and automobiles. When you put the sucker on the stone, being wet and floppy it fits on the stone so exactly that there is no air between the leather and the stone, but there's lots of air pressing down on top of the sucker. That holds the sucker to the stone and when you pull up, there's still air pressing down on the sucker, to hold it to the stone. The sucker is, we say, sticking to the stone.

What you're doing when you use a rubber suction cup is push on it so that there's no air under it, but of course there's air on top of it, so it sticks the same way.

The trick in making a leather sucker is to make sure that the hole in the center is no larger than the string, because if it is, air will get in, and it won't work.

Now, I'm sending you to the library again. If you have some leather left over, and if you have found out you like fooling around with leather, you can find a book in the library that will tell you how to make all sorts of things out of leather.

If you have a horse chestnut tree somewhere in your neighborhood, there's a game we used to play every fall when we were kids that I'm going to tell you about. You'll need another kid to play with, but as far as getting ready for the game is concerned, you can do that yourself. Once again, if you don't know what a horse chestnut tree looks like, ask somebody or look in the library book that I told you about when I told you about willow whistles.

In the fall, on a horse chestnut tree you'll see things called burrs.

They're like the burrs you use to make burr baskets in that they're prickly, but they're quite different. They're about the size of an apricot, they're green, and they hang from the branches in clusters. Depending on what time of the year you go looking for a horse chestnut tree and what part of the country you live in, you'll find them hanging from the tree or lying on the ground around the base of the tree. If you'll spilt them open, you'll find a horse chestnut inside.

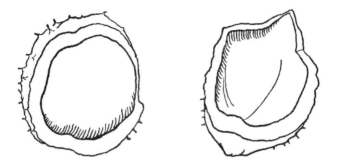

Sometimes you'll find them half open and you can just pull the two halves of the burr apart with your fingers, sometimes they're still so green you may have to stamp on the burr with your heel until it splits. If the horse chestnuts are ready to use, they'll be brown, a real wonderful glossy brown.

If you split a couple of burrs open and find they're white, or part white and part brown, or very light brown, you'll have to go away for a day or two and try again.

Now let's say you've waited and you've got a bunch of horse chestnuts. By the way, when we were kids, the horse chestnut tree in my neighborhood was on a neighbor's lawn. It might be a good idea to ask if you can go get them, if your horse chestnut tree is on a neighbor's lawn.

Not that anyone wants them but kids, but the ones you can't reach, you'll jump for, and if that doesn't do it, you'll shy a branch up into the tree to knock them down, and if the neighbor has just invested three million dollars in new grass seed, he may not like having it all covered over with branches and burrs and kids. But I'm sure he won't be a grouch about it. Chances are when he was a kid he did the same thing, and you'll come home with as many horse chestnuts as you can carry. I don't have to tell you to look at them, because they're the nicest things in the world to look at, and you'll be doing that anyway. If you want them to shine more, take them and rub them up against the side

of your nose. Perhaps you've seen your father or someone do that with a pipe. There's oil on everybody's skin there and it oils up the chestnut or the pipe and makes it shine.

Okay, now you have some horse chestnuts, and they're fun to get and fun to open the burrs and fun to look at and fun to shine. There are things you can *do* with horse chestnuts, too.

You can't eat them, at least I never could, but here's a game you can play with them. This, like mumbly-peg, is a game you need another kid to play with, but getting the horse chestnuts ready is something you can do by yourself. Pick out the ones that look good and solid. Now, bore a hole right through them, through the center of that rough, woody little part right through to the other side. You can do this with the mumbly-peg blade of your Scout knife, or with a long nail. We used to do it with an ice-pick, but I imagine a lot of you have never seen or heard of an ice-pick. When I was a kid it was darn near the handiest tool in the house. That was before electric refrigerators, and the way we used to keep food cool was, a man came in a horse and wagon every other day, or even every day in the summer. In the back of his wagon were great big chunks of ice, as tall as I was when I was little. He would ask my mother how much ice she wanted. She'd tell him a fifty-pound piece or a hundred-pound piece, and he'd take out his ice-pick—it was just a long sharp steel point set in a handle—and he'd chip a little line along the great big piece of ice and like magic, the big piece would break right along the line and there would be a fifty-pound piece. In the summer, we'd always wait for the ice man because when the ice split there'd be pieces of ice just the right size for putting in your mouth. Then he'd take a tongs that looked like this,

jab both points in the ice, and sling the fifty-pound piece of ice up on his shoulder. He had a kind of leather pad up there. He'd carry it into the house and put it in the ice-box, just a big wooden chest with a door on the front. That's what kept the food cool.

Robert Paul Smith

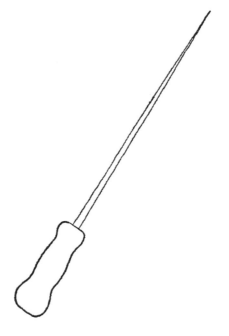

Well, each house had an ice-pick too, in case you wanted a smaller piece of ice, for putting in a pitcher of water or lemonade or something. So we always knew where the ice-pick was, right on the side of the ice box, and when we wanted to drill holes in horse chestnuts or belts or whatever, we went looking for the ice-pick.

You see, we didn't always know where our Scout knife was—if we had one—any more than you do.

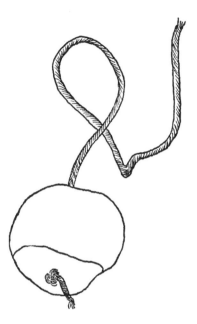

Well, so you bore a hole in your horse chestnuts. Then you get a piece of strong string. An old shoelace is good, if you have an old shoelace. Thread the string through the horse chestnut, tie a couple of good hard knots on the bottom of the string so that the horse chestnut slides to the bottom of the string and stays there.

All you need is the one string, and the reason why I suggested a shoelace is because from time to time you're going to have to put a new horse chestnut on the string, and the stiff tip on a shoelace makes the threading easy.

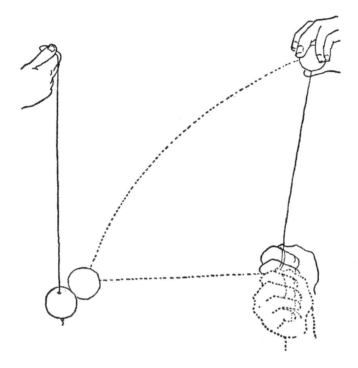

We called the game killers. I am told that they play it in England and call it conkers, and somebody once told me that some places in England they play it with snail shells, too, but I don't know anything about that.

Let's say you find another kid, and either show him how to get a horse chestnut and thread it on a string, or let him get his own string and lend him a chestnut to start with.

You choose up for who goes first. The one who loses holds the end of his string with the horse chestnut dangling down. Say you've won the choosing up: you take the end of your string in one hand, the chestnut in the other. (All through this book, I've been saying right hand and left hand, but since a lot of you are left-handed, I'm just going to say one hand or the other from here on. When I was a kid I was left-handed, and now I'm more or less right-handed, so I know how confusing it can be.) The idea is to swing your killer down so it hits the other kid's. It may take you a while to get the idea, but it's not hard to do.

Then you hold up your killer and he gets a shot at yours. The idea is to break his killer. After a certain number of shots, you'll see a crack in his killer, or in yours, or in both. You keep on until one breaks, so that it can no longer stay on the string. Sometimes it happens that you bust your own killer in hitting his; that still means you lose. The kid who has the killer left on the string, no matter how it happens, is the winner. That's the game. Now if your killer breaks his, it's a one-killer. If it breaks another one of his, or one of another kid's, it's a two-killer, and so on.

I can't be sure about this next part, but I think that if a one-killer busted a six-killer, it then became a seven-killer. All I can remember for sure is that once I had a forty-killer.

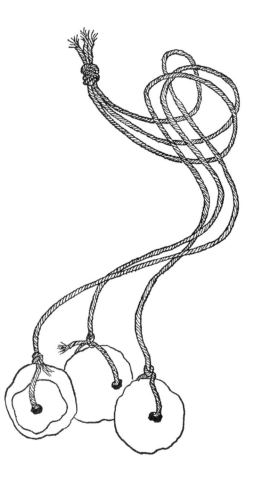

If you get tired of this game, and still have some horse chestnuts left, you can make what we called *bolas*. That's a Spanish word, and Mitch read somewhere that in Argentina, instead of a lasso, the gauchos, the Argentine cowboys, used *bolas*. Theirs are made of rawhide and metal balls, but we made ours of horse chestnuts and string. You get three horse chestnuts and fasten each one of them to a string, oh, about two feet long. Put the string through and tie it on around so that the horse chestnuts will stay at the end of the string. Now take the other ends of the string and tie them all together.

Now, if you will take this by one horse chestnut and whirl it around your head and let it go so that it's aiming at a tree, when you hit the tree with any of the horse chestnuts the string will wrap around and so will the other horse chestnuts. The gauchos used them to wrap around the legs of cattle to hold them, instead of a lasso. What animals you use them on is your affair.

I'm not sure that we called these next things bull-roarers when we made them as kids, but I've since found out that's what they're called. I've also found out that they make them in many parts of the world, and in some primitive tribes, they're used by the grownups to scare devils away. We just used them to make enough noise to drive grownups away.

These are a cinch to make. You need two pieces of wood and a piece of string. It really doesn't matter what size you make these either, but a good size to start with is one piece of wood about a foot long and half an inch square, another piece about two and a half inches wide, six inches long and a quarter of an inch thick. The first piece is just to be used as a handle, so make it any size that will fit your hand. The other piece has to be thin, but if it's a *little* more or less than a quarter-inch thick, it doesn't make any difference. All you do is bore a hole in one end of the handle, and in the middle of the end of the flat piece. Thread a piece of string about six inches long through the hole in the handle, and tie a good hard knot so it won't come through. Do the same thing with the other end of the string, through the hole in the flat piece. That's the whole thing, all the making you have to do.

Now, whirl it around, holding it by the end of the handle, and when it gets going fast enough, the flat piece will whirl from the air hitting it, and it will start making a wonderful noise. It will work even better if you make both sides of the thin piece taper to an edge, like a knife blade. Whirl it faster and the noise gets higher, whirl it slower and the noise gets lower. You have now learned, even if you don't know it yet, something about the science of physics. I won't tell you what it is, but later on, when you

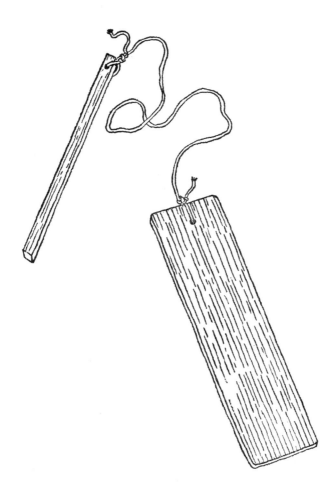

study science, or right now, if you are studying science, you'll find out. The reason I won't tell you is because if I don't, maybe you'll go to your library again and get out a

book about elementary physics, and that'll be one other
nothing you can do with nobody.

You probably have seen or heard of boomerangs; they
were invented by another primitive people, in Australia,
and everybody thinks that what a boomerang is is a thing
that you throw and it comes back to you. The fact of the
matter is that what the Australian natives did mostly was
make bent sticks that they could throw to hit game with,
and the idea of it coming back to them was found out, like
all great discoveries, by accident. Much later on, they
started making them deliberately to come back, and the
boomerangs that you see now are just for sport, for fun.
You can buy them in a store, they make them of wood and,
I understand, now, of plastic. I owned a wooden one when
I grew up: a friend of mine gave me one for a present, and
I took it along with me on a vacation. One day my wife and
I walked out into a big open field; I had no belief I could
throw it and make it come back to me, and I told my wife
we'd better get ready for a long hike across the field to pick
it up, and then I rared back and threw it. It went an awful
long ways, and I was just saying to my wife, "You see, I
never believed they really work," when all of a sudden I

heard a whistling noise, looked up, and ducked out of the way just in time to see the boomerang stick in the ground about three inches from where my foot had just been. I was immediately convinced that I was a natural born boomeranger, or whatever they call them. I rared back and let fly again. It didn't come back. I had a nice long walk across the field. I rared back again. Same thing. I never did get it to work that well again.

But when we were kids, we never made that kind of boomerang. In the past couple of years, there have been articles in magazines and maybe in some books, about how to make that kind, but I think it's quite a job, unless you're really good at woodworking. If you want that kind of boomerang, maybe your shop teacher can help you out.

In the meantime, here are two different kinds that are easy to make. One is an indoor boomerang. Okay, now you're sure that I have gone completely goofy, but that's what I mean. An indoor boomerang. Get a piece of very thin cardboard. If your father uses business cards, that's exactly the right kind of cardboard, and the right size. The top flap of a matchbook will do, too. Now just cut a boomerang shape out of it, just about the same size and shape as in the drawing. Now put it on a book, so that one arm sticks out just a little bit.

Flick it with your fingernail and it'll go sailing out just like an Australian boomerang, and after very little practice, you'll find out how to make it whirl so that it will come back to you. A good way to do it is to hold the book in one hand, tipped up a little, so that the boomerang goes up in the air at an angle, and slides back at just about the same angle, like a ball going almost to the top of a hill, and then rolling down again.

The other kind of boomerang is for use outdoors, and all you need for it is two long strips of thin wood, about the size of a regular twelve-inch ruler. Balsa wood, that you can get at a hobby shop, is good for this, but any light, thin wood is good, like the sides of an orange crate, which you can pick up for free at the grocer's or the supermarket. All you do is make a cross of the two pieces, and fasten them together with a small rubber band. A good way to do this is to put the rubber band on one piece, a little way from the top.

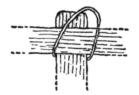

Cross the other piece over, between the rubber band and the end of the first piece, then pull the rubber band up over the second piece and around and under the first piece.

As always, if the rubber band is too long, double it.

Then slide the second piece down until it's in the center.

Take the cross-boomerang outside and throw it so that it spins, and so that it's heading up at an angle into the air. It'll whirl, and come back to you. You can round the corners, or paint it, or nail the two pieces together, if you like.

The next thing on my list is umbrella bows and arrows, but when my own kids saw the list, and I started telling them what it was, I found out something upsetting. An umbrella bow and arrow is something you make out of an old busted umbrella, and I haven't seen an old busted umbrella for a long time. I got to thinking about it, because when I was a kid, it was a fairly common thing. There was a kind of shopping we used to do when we were kids, which was just walking down our block and seeing what people had thrown away in the trash can, and taking out those things that looked useful. Quite often, in one of the trash cans was a busted umbrella, and whoever saw it first grabbed it. Come to think of it, it must have driven our mothers nuts. Let's say Mrs. Horn threw away a busted umbrella. Well, if I happened to see it before Charlie Horn, I hooked it, and carried it back to my house, and later on Charlie Horn came by, and I gave him part of the umbrella, and he took it home, and then later my mother put what I left of the umbrella in our trash can and Charlie Horn saw it, and he took what was left home, and then my mother threw away *her* busted umbrella and then Charlie Horn came along and hooked it, and—well, the way I figure it, nobody ever really got rid of any trash on our block. It just kind of got moved around from house to house.

I can think of a number of reasons why you don't see busted umbrellas any more. In the first place, in our town, we don't put trash cans on the street, so a busted umbrella might be harder to locate. But I don't think that's the main reason. In those days, the olden days, umbrellas were made of cotton, or, if you were rich, silk. And people used to walk a lot more then, because there weren't so many cars, and the umbrellas got used more, and cotton and silk, after a while, rot. Nowadays, umbrellas aren't used so much, and I imagine they're made out of nylon, and that doesn't rot.

But if, after all this, you do happen to run across a busted umbrella, the first thing to do is to get all that remains of the cloth off the ribs, and then pry the ribs loose from the center part. You can use brute strength, pliers, or intelligence. The thing is to get them loose. Now, right there you have made something: what you have left is a very useful cane.

If you tie a piece of thin strong cord, like fishline, to one end of one rib, pull the cord tight and tie it to the other end, you've got a bow. And if by this time, you're strong enough to bend down and pick up one of the other ribs, you've got an arrow. The arrows are pretty sharp, so one more time I'll say anybody who shoots a gun, bow and arrow, dart, slingshot, *anything*, at another kid is a dope, and I'd just as lief he didn't read this book.

I just now mentioned a slingshot, and I don't suppose I have to tell you how to make one out of a forked branch, but just in case you don't know, all there is to it is to look around (in the fall is a good time, because you can see the branches clearly with the leaves gone) for a good strong forked twig. Cut the two ends even, and the handle to your hand size, so it looks like a capital Y.

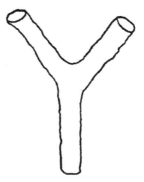

Get a good strong rubber band, cut it so it's one long piece. Get a soft piece of leather, and cut it to this shape.

Thread the rubber band through the holes in the leather. Wrap each end of the rubber band once around each end of the Y and tie it with good strong cord.

Pebbles or nuts or beans are your ammunition.

If you live in the city and have trouble finding a forked twig, you can saw out a wood fork; we found out that this shape was maybe even better than the forked twig.

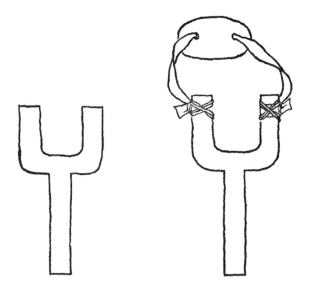

And if you don't have the wood and the saw, if your mother or father ever bring home a package with one of those wood-and-wire carrying handles, like this,

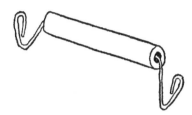

get a pliers, straighten out the wire and pull it right through the hollow handle. Then twist it into a fork shape and push it back into the handle and make your slingshot. This kind, you can just tie the ends onto the wire.

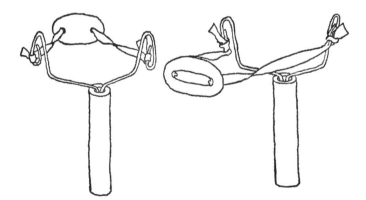

For some reason, when I was a kid, I used to like to make things very small—perhaps you do, too—and I used to make a little tiny slingshot out of a hairpin. If your mother uses hairpins, you know what they're shaped like. Well, all you have to do is bend it like a slingshot, and using just a plain, everyday, little rubber band and a piece of cloth instead of the leather, and thread instead of the string, you've got a miniature slingshot. I made a lot of them, and took them to school with me, and I guess my teacher liked to shoot miniature slingshots, too, because she made a collection of mine.*

There's still another kind of slingshot, sort of a cross between a slingshot and a bow and arrow, that you can make out of a spool. All you do is cut a wide rubber band at one end, and tie the two ends onto a spool. If the hole in

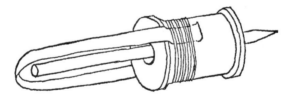

the spool is big enough, you can use pencils for arrows, if it isn't, use lollipop sticks, or any straight stick that will fit

---

* I hear tell hairpins are pretty rare now. Maybe you can make them out of bobby-pins, but I don't know about this.

with a little room to spare into the hole in the spool. Grab the pencil or the stick between the sides of the rubber band, pull back and let go.

There's a kind of gun you can make, too, with rubber bands. The simplest way to make one is just to cut a piece of wood, somewhere between a quarter of an inch and half an inch thick, into a pistol shape. On the top, just jam the point of your knife in so that it makes a flat hole. Then cut a piece of cardboard into little half-inch squares. Put a rubber band on the gun, a rubber band big enough so that when you pull it back over the top of the handle, it's good and stretched. You can put a thumbtack through the rubber band where it comes over the front end of the pistol. Now jam one of the little cardboard squares into the flat hole, like this.

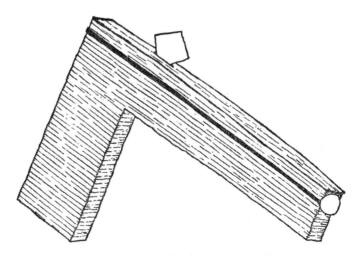

Now if you'll hold the gun, you'll find that by rubbing your thumb up, you'll push the rubber band up over the end of the handle and it will spring forward and flick the card.

I just now thought that maybe if you've made the cardboard boomerang, you could probably fit one of those into the crack, hold the gun sideways, and it would probably flick the boomerang better than a finger.

If you've got a lot of rubber bands, you can make the card gun into an automatic rubber-band gun. Just loop the rubber bands over and release them one at a time with your thumb.

If you don't have any rubber bands, you can make the real old-fashioned kind of sling, the kind David used on Goliath. All you need for this is some string and a piece of cloth or leather. Make the sling just the way you made the rubber-band part of the slingshot, using string instead of rubber, and make the strings longer.

We used to use acorns or horse chestnuts for ammunition, because we never got to control these slings very well. Put an acorn in the cloth or leather—here's really the only part that's different from the slingshot: when you tie the strings, try to make the cloth or leather into a little pouch—hold the ends of the string and whirl it around

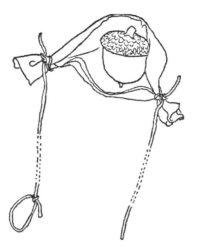

your head. When you've got some speed up, let go of one of the strings, and the acorn will fly. Don't expect to hit things the way you do with a slingshot right away, or even ever. It takes a lot of practice to get this one going right, and we were never able to get nearly as accurate with this as with a slingshot.

If you live out in the country, you probably know about whipping apples, but if you don't, or if you only go to the country for vacations, here's the way it goes. What you need is a long, whippy branch or switch, and an apple tree that nobody's paying any attention to, like the one in my back yard. You'll find apples on the ground, either green or a little squishy. Sharpen the end of the switch, stick it into the apple, bring your arm back and throw, sort of like casting a fishline. I think you'll be amazed at how far you can throw this way, much faster than just throwing with your hand. It's sort of like having an arm six feet long. I guess you could do this with any fruit or nut that was soft enough to stick on the end of a branch, if you don't run across an apple tree that nobody's paying any attention to in your part of the country. If you find some clay, and mold it into balls, they work well, too.

The Indians used this same idea to make throwing sticks. There are darn near as many ways of making throwing sticks as there were Indians, but the idea of all of them is the same, and it's the same as whipping apples, a way of making your arm longer.

The general idea is to make a stick with a bump, a hook, or a nail in it.

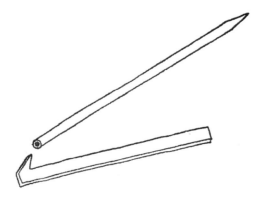

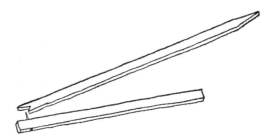

Then make an arrow to put on the bump or hook or nail.

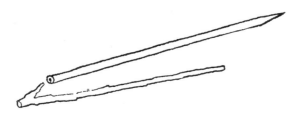

You hold the throwing stick with your hand bent back, the arrow lying along the top of the stick. Whip it forward the same way as you would do with the apple whip or a fishing pole, so that as you throw the throwing stick comes up and over and releases the arrow. You can make these any way you like; you can put points on the arrow with a nail or by sharpening it, you can put feathers on the back—and you'll find it's a whole lot easier if you don't use feathers, but make a slot and make the feather-vanes out of cardboard or thin wood.

Like the old-fashioned sling, this one takes a little doing, but the Indians used it; lots of tribes never used bows and arrows at all, but throwing sticks all the time. No, I'm not that old. I didn't know any Indians, except once a year, one used to come to our school and give a speech. It is my recollection that he was the Indian whose face you'll see on an old Indian Head nickel. He never said one mumbling thing about throwing sticks. To tell you the truth, I don't know what he talked about at all. I just know he came to the school every year, and said the same thing every year.

I don't know how old you are, and I really don't know any more how old I was when I did the different things in this book, so if you find that some of the things are too old for you—wait until you're old enough to do them. If you find that some of the things in the book are too young for you, first figure out if they're really too young, if nobody else knows that you're doing them. I know that when I was a grown man, my wife and I went to live in Mexico for a while, and walking down the street one day, I saw a whole bunch of kids playing with what was, for me, a brand new toy. It was a yo-yo, and I'd never seen one before. I bought one—I told the shopkeeper that it was for my kid, but I didn't have a kid then, and I brought it home with me. Now certainly a yo-yo, as a matter of fact *any* toy, was too young for a man almost thirty years old, so I used to sneak out in the back yard when I wanted to learn how to use a yo-yo, and any time anybody came to the house when I was doing it, I stuck it in my pocket and pretended that I had been out back doing something important and grownup.

So, first of all, remember that the name of this book is *How to Do Nothing with Nobody All Alone by Yourself* and if some of the things sound a little childish, figure it out: do you think they're too childish, or do *you* think that if someone else saw you doing it, *he* would think it was childish? And if you really are too old to do some of these things, why don't you show your kid brother how to do them, or your little sister, or any little kid on the block? He or she or they will think they're great things, and they'll think you're great for showing them.

Take, for example, polly-noses. You know how, in the fall, those little wing things fall off the maple trees. They look like this.

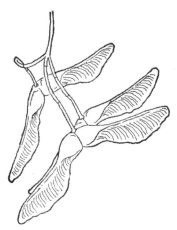

First of all, if you'll get up on a fairly high place and just drop one, you'll see some real flying. Then, after you get down from the high place, if you'll separate the two wings at the joint, you'll see that the base of each half is sort of double. If you'll stick your fingernail in between the two halves and pull them apart a little,

you'll find that there's some sticky stuff that lines this place, and if you put it on your nose, it'll stay there and you'll have what we called a polly-nose. Polly was what we called a parrot, and somehow we thought that with these on, our noses looked something like parrots' beaks.

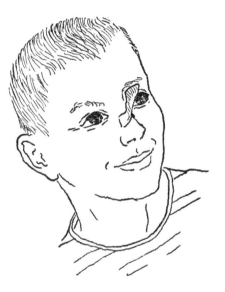

Silly? You bet. But sometimes it's fun to be silly, and didn't you laugh just the other night when the man on television put on a funny hat?

That reminds me of another kind of silly thing we did. We called it owl-eyes. You need another kid, or a docile parent, for this. Put your nose up against his, and your forehead up against his. Both of you close your eyes, one of you or both of you count, "One, two, three, owl-eyes." As you say "three," both of you open your eyes at the same moment, and I'll guarantee you'll see owl-eyes. I just got to wondering what would happen if you did this all alone, by pressing your nose up against a mirror instead of another kid. I went and tried it, just this minute. It works, so this *is* something you can do all by yourself.

In the summer, in my part of the country, late in the summer and right on into the fall, there's a plant growing all over the place wherever there's a brook or a stream or a lake. It's called jewel weed, and it's easy to find by looking for the orange flower. It's a real pretty plant, and in the late summer and early fall, in addition to the flowers there's a little green pod that grows on it. It looks like a tiny green banana.

Well, if you find the plant, and if you find the pod, and if you squeeze it *very* gently, you'll find out that it may look like a tiny green banana, but it behaves more like a tiny green banana-shaped bomb.

I'm sure all of you have seen pussy willow one time or another, and I'll bet a hat that there isn't one of you, really, who at one time or another hasn't stroked one of the buds, because they're so exactly like a kitten's fur. Here's one of the things I did when I was a kid that I don't think I would

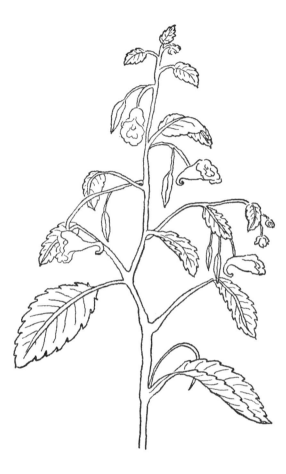

have liked another kid to watch me doing. It seemed a little childish to me. But I did it, and I had fun doing it, all
the same. You can take a knife, and slice right through one
pussy willow the long way. Get a little piece of paper, and
glue that half down. Then cut the tip of the other half of

the bud, the short way. If you glue that on the paper right next to the first one, can you see what you've started to make? Looks sort of like a bee, doesn't it. Well, with a pencil or a pen, draw in the legs. You can make it as simple or complicated as you like; you can—here we go again—go to the library and see what a bee really looks like, or you can go take a good look at a real bee, if there are any around, and you can make the pussy-willow bee just like the real one.

Or, if you like, cut wings out of cellophane or paper, and make up a new kind of bug. Maybe you'll have an idea how to make a totally different kind of animal. A lady was telling me the other day that when she was a kid, they used to draw a fence on the paper, glue the pussy willows on, draw tails and whiskers—and there you have pussy-willow cats sitting on a fence.

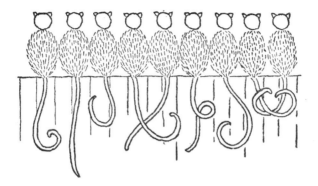

I know this sounds goofy, but if you can get a piece of wood and ten pins you can make a piano. Oh, not a big piano like the one you have. You'd need a lot more wood and pins for that. This is a pin-piano, and it's a musical instrument, and it plays very *piano*. The word piano means soft. The real name for a piano is pianoforte, and all it means is an instrument that can play loud or soft. Well, this is a pin-piano and it just plays soft. All you do is stick the pins into the piece of wood, each one a little further in than that first one.

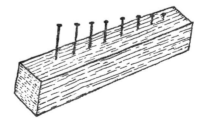

If you take a nail and hit the pin, you'll hear a certain note. By pushing the next pin in a little further, you'll hear a higher note. And so on. Tune as you go, "do re mi fa sol la ti do." But that's only eight pins. Why did I say ten? Because you're going to bend at least two of the pins trying to get them in to the right depth. We always did.

When we were kids, we read in books about making cigar-box guitars and fiddles, but I must say they were never very successful, and these days, most cigar boxes I run across are made out of heavy cardboard. That's a shame, because the cedar wood they were made of was just the right size and thickness to make all sorts of things out of wood, and in addition, cedar wood has such a wonderful smell. Coupled with the cigar smell, it was just about the best smell in the world. But some cigars are still packed in cedar boxes, and if you can get ahold of them, you'll find the wood just the right thing to make many of the things in this book. Also, they're held together with little tiny nails which are just the right size for cigar-box wood, to go through and not split. The way to get the paper off is to let the wood soak in water until the paste is dissolved, after you've carefully taken the box apart and saved the nails. You can hold the wood under water by putting something heavy on top of it. If you do it in the washbasin in your bathroom, the handiest heavy thing is your tooth-brushing glass filled with water. Once the paper is soaked off, it's sometimes a good idea to put the wood to dry between paper towels or newspaper, with a heavy book on top, to keep the wood from warping.

As I say, the cigar-box fiddles we made never worked very well, but I can tell you an easy way to make a musical instrument that works. I know it does, because I made one a couple of months ago for one of my kids. Get a big empty tin can, the kind that has a top that comes off all in one piece, like a coffee can, or maybe, like me, you'll be lucky enough to find an old beat-up canister that your mother's through with, the kind that she keeps flour or coffee or sugar or salt in, the kind that has a lid that fits. I don't really think it's even important whether it has a lid on it, but that's what I used and it works pretty well. I also found an old yardstick a paint store had given me, but any long thin flexible piece of wood will do. Punch a hole in the top of the can. You can do this by using a nail and a hammer. Get a piece of thin wire; if you or someone in your family or one of your friends plays the guitar or the mandolin or the ukulele or the violin, and they've got an old music string they don't need any more, that will do fine. Whichever you get, tie a knot in one end of it, or

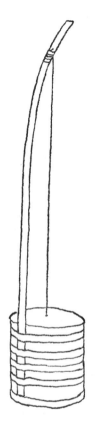

if it's too stiff to knot, tie it around a little piece of wood, so that you can thread it through the hole and pull rightly on it, without it coming through the hole. Now take the yardstick and drill a hole in that, too. Take the other end of the yardstick and put it against the side of the can, wind around the can with masking tape or adhesive tape or any strong sticky tape you have. Now bend the yardstick like a bow, but just a little ways, and thread the other end of the wire through the hole, and fasten that end of the wire down with tape, or tie a knot in it, any way you like so that the wire keeps the yardstick bent in a bow.

If you'll pluck the string, holding the whole thing by the yardstick in your closed hand, bending the yardstick into more or less of a bow, you'll produce a kind of ba-*voom* noise, which sounds very much like some of the noises you've heard on television when the man with the checkered suit has had one drink too many. You can also, by bending the yardstick more or less, play a tune on this— more or less. If you want to try different things, just take a rough stick and use it for a bow, like playing the violin, instead of plucking, and you can get a still different kind of noise by hitting the string with a stick while you bend the yardstick back and forth. I don't know what the name of this is. It's just a ba-*voom* thing.

If you live in the part of the country where they grow lots of corn, I've been told and I've seen pictures of a thing that looks wonderful to me; a cornstalk fiddle. Where I grew up, they didn't raise corn, and so we never made them, so I can't tell you how, but maybe your father or your uncle or your grandfather knows.

While you're talking to your grandfather, maybe he still knows how to carve peach-pit monkeys. My grandfather did, and he also knew how to get the whole peel off an apple in one long strip every time. It's pretty hard to do, making a peach-pit monkey, so hard I'm not sure a book can tell you how to do it. I know it's too hard for me to tell you in a book, but I can tell you how to make a peach-pit basket, and a peach-pit fish, and a peach-pit turtle. Save the peach pits as you eat them, and get them as clean as you can by gnawing, and by pulling out the little threads that are left with your fingers. When you've got it as clean as you can, put it away and let it dry. Since peaches come in the summer, and carving things from peach pits is an indoor thing that you can do in the winter, leave them until they're really dry. When they are, pick out a good big one to start, because it's tricky work at best, and the bigger the pit, the easier for beginners. My guess is that if you have any tools at all, you have a coping saw. (Maybe you call it a jig saw.) With the saw, make one cut, just on the side of the little ridge, from the pointy end of the peach pit to about half way down. Then another cut, same way, on the other side of the ridge. Then another cut from the side of the peach pit to the first cut, same on the other side, so that your peach pit looks like this from the narrow side.

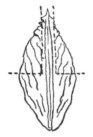

Turn the peach pit to one wide side, and then the other, and look at it. On one side or the other, and sometimes both, you'll see just the tip of what looks like an almond. If you poke it with the tip of the smallest blade in your knife, you'll find it's soft, even softer than an almond, and you can pick it out, a little crumb at a time, or if the peach pits happen to be accommodating, out to help you, sometimes you can get the whole almond thing out in one piece.

It is *not* an almond, by the way, and we used to think it was poison, and for all I know, maybe it is. I do know it isn't good for you to eat. It tastes pretty bad, even worse than acorns, and they were terrible.

Anyhow, you can see now the beginning of the basket. The part up on top is the little handle, the bottom is the basket part.

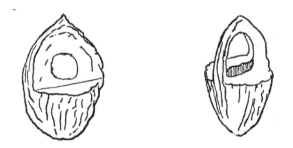

You'll find that the reason some people call a peach pit a peach stone is because it's darn near as hard as a stone, and to open up the hole to make a real good handle means chipping off the inside of the loop, one tiny little sliver at a time. I might as well tell you now, you'll probably break two for every one you make, especially as you get better and try to make the handle thinner and thinner, more like a real basket. You can smooth off the outside, too, with sandpaper, or by rubbing it on cement like the clamshell bracelets. It takes a long long time. I guess I better tell you, if you're not the kind of kid who's got an awful lot of patience, don't try peach-pit baskets.

The way you make turtles is all with a knife, just cutting from the outside, like this. The reason for making the turtle at all is that the markings on the peach pit, when you start to grind it down, look something like a turtle shell.

The fish the same way.

A little ways back, I was talking about wooden cigar boxes, and what I always made out of the long thin strip that had

been the front of the box was a paddle-wheel boat. Just cut out a boat shape on the front, and cut out a piece with your coping saw in back. Cut two little notches on the end pieces, smooth up the edges of the piece you cut out. Put a rubber band from notch to notch, put the piece you cut out halfway through the rubber band.

Wind it, hold it tight, put it in the water. It goes.

You can fancy this up any way you like, putting a little cabin on the deck, or a mast, and if you can cut two little pieces of wood,

you can fit the notch of one into the notch of the other,

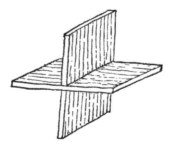

and put that in the rubber band, and have a four-blade paddle wheel.

It would be my guess that all of you know how to make airplanes (some people call them darts) out of a piece of paper. In case you don't, you fold the paper lengthwise, open it out, then fold the two ends in like this,

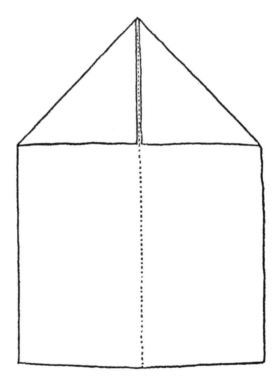

so what used to be the top of the paper now lies along the center fold. Now fold the two sides together to make sure that everything's even, open it out again and fold again,

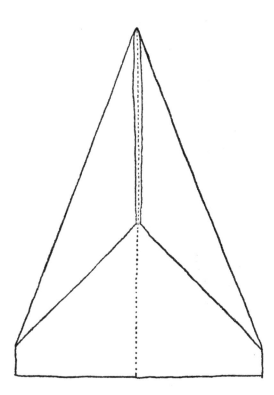

so that the two new folded sides lie along the center fold.

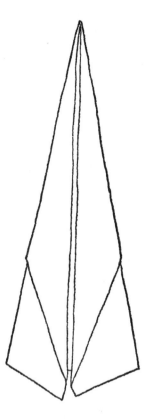

Fold these two halves together and then fold back the two thick pieces the other way so that the folded part lies even with the bottom.

We used to take the bottom and tear back through the thick part, to make two little tabs, one going one way, the other the other, to sort of hold the whole thing together.

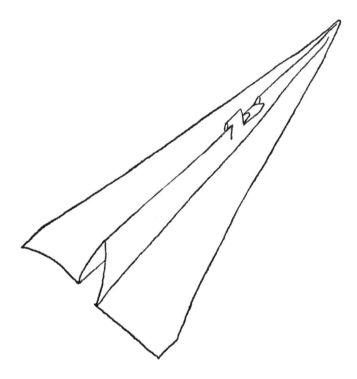

Teachers used to take these away from us, too.

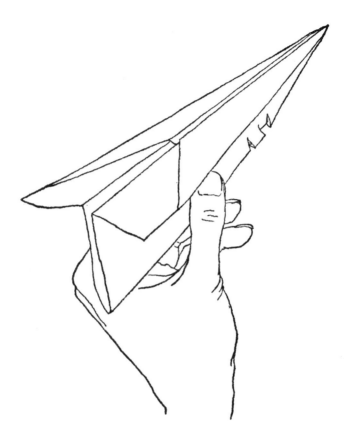

Then I used to make a different kind; it's my recollection that I invented this kind, but chances are that's just my memory, and I probably saw it in a book or learned it from another kid. Anyhow, the idea was to make a paper airplane that looked more like an airplane. You start off the same way, folding down the center and opening up, folding the two ends in.

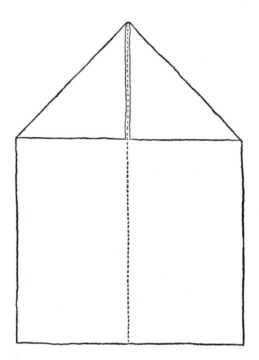

Then you take the point and bend it back so that the very point evens up with the cross line.

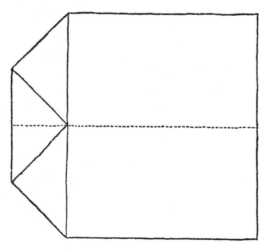

Fold the whole thing over,

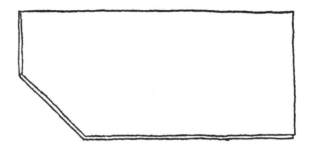

and then fold back the two wings a little ways up from the first original center fold. Fold it back in half again and with scissors, or by tearing, make an airplane shape, like this.

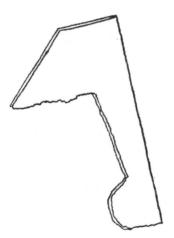

Now fold the wings out, and fold the little tail pieces out. Make the tear and make the tab like before.

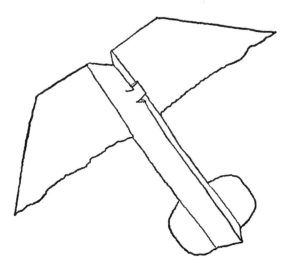

These fly much more like an airplane than the old kind, and you can even experiment with bending the tail pieces

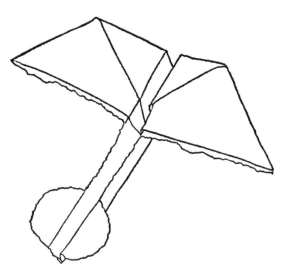

up to make the plane loop the loop, or one side up to make it go in a circle. Just generally, with these or with gliders that you can get at an airplane model store, to make a plane loop the loop, throw it down, to make it go in a circle and come back to you, hold it in your right hand if you're right-handed, your left if you're left-handed, with the bottom of the plane toward you and the wings straight up and down and sort of sweep it backhanded right across your own front.

There's a way of making a helicopter, too. By the way, when I was a kid, it was clearly understood that there never would ever be a real full-size, man-carrying helicopter. It had been very carefully proven, scientifically, that it was impossible ever to make one that would get off the ground. I don't know what happened to the scientists who proved this: maybe they met the scientist who had proved that, by all the laws of nature, it was impossible for a bee to fly. A bee just wasn't made right to fly. I'm not making fun of scientists; it wasn't so long ago that all the scientific theories in the world were based on the theory that it was impossible to split the atom. Well, of course. Everything is impossible until it's done. Then whatever has been done is possible, and there's a new thing that's impossible.

The helicopters we made weren't really helicopters. They just looked something like what we now know as helicopters. They were made from a piece of paper, and they worked very much the same way as the maple wings I told you about when I was telling about polly-noses. Take a piece of stiff paper or thin cardboard, the size isn't important, and cut it to this shape.

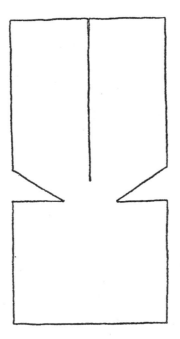

Bend the wings back, and fold over the bottom part so that the bottom part is three thicknesses thick, and glue it or staple it or paper-clip it.

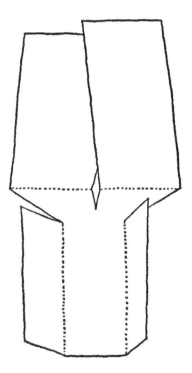

Take this up to a high place, and let it drop.

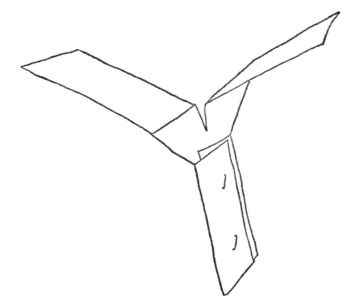

If you can get a hold of a chicken or a turkey wishbone, some chewing gum, a burnt kitchen match and a rubber band, you can make a kind of silly thing. You chew this wishbone good and clean, and if you've got the patience, let it dry until it's good and stiff. Chew the gum until it's good and chewy. Take a little wad of it and stick it on the wishbone where there's that flat place. (If you live on a tarred street and the tar gets sticky in the summer, tar is even better for this than chewing gum.*) Loop the rubber band over the two arms of the wishbone, out near the end,

* That stuff called silly putty works, too, but that costs money.

put a match in between the rubber band,

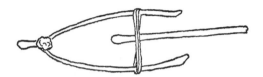

twist it up good so that if you let it go it would whirl around to the other side of the wishbone and be stopped, only don't let it go.

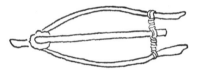

Stick the end of the match into the chewing gum and set the whole thing down on a table.

After a little while the twisted rubber band will pull the match away from the chewing gum and the whole thing will pop up in the air. Of course, you never know how long it's going to take for the match to come loose. I'll guarantee only one thing; it won't ever let loose at the exact moment you're expecting it. If you put it on the table next to your father when he's making out his income-tax return, it should produce some interesting results. He may tell you what he did to scare his father when he was a kid, and he may even show you what his father did to him when he scared him when he was a kid.

There are lots of other things you can do, all alone, by yourself, but these are about all I can think of right now that aren't specialized in some way.

I'm really serious about the library: that's the best place to learn more. We did lots of other things when we were kids, like collecting bugs, and wild flowers, and frogs, and snakes, and stones—and in the library I promise you there will be a really expert book on each of these, and on many other subjects, written by people who've made a life study of those special things. There will be books about trees and radio sets and telescopes and badminton and Indian crafts and metal work, about how to make bows and arrows, how to swim, how to—oh, there's no end. There's even a book on how to find a how-to book.

Some silly grownup has even written a book on how to read a book.

But if you've gotten this far, I know you know how to read a book.

There's only one thing left to tell you: the name of this book is *How to Do Nothing with Nobody All Alone by Yourself.* I understand some people get worried about kids who spend a lot of time all alone, by themselves. I do a little worrying about that, but I worry about something else even more; about kids who don't know how to spend any time all alone, by themselves. It's something you're going to be doing a whole lot of, no matter what, for the rest of your lives. And I think it's a good thing to do; you get to know yourself, and I think that's the most important thing in the whole world.

Index

Acknowledgments

Thanks are due my wife, who drew the pictures, and my sons Dan and Joe, who helped me make all the things in the book for her to draw.